Neuroscientific Design!

ROBERT S. MURPHY

Deeper Understanding Books

All graphics and layouts by Robert S. Murphy
Optimal Levels! is based on CREAME pedagogy
(Consciousness Raising, Emotions Analysis, Manipulation, and Expression)

CREAME and *Optimal Levels!* designed by Robert S. Murphy

About this series

Welcome to the **OPTIMAL LEVELS!** series. This series is probably unlike any series of textbooks that you have encountered in the past. These textbooks have been designed to maximize student thinking and foster the construction of cognitive skills through the usage of the English language. This series is based upon my own research in *Mind, Brain, and Education* at Harvard University and my Master's research in TEFL/TESL at the University of Birmingham.

You will find no rote memorization tasks here -and there are no grammar boxes either! *"Deeper Understanding"* is really about the ability to solve puzzles and problems in the real world. Memorization tasks and grammar boxes have little impact on dynamically changing real world issues. Rather than *presenting* to students what must be learned, this series proposes motivating themes and scaffolded tasks that are designed to build skills <u>dynamically</u>. By doing the theme-based student-centered tasks, students dynamically learn and understand language usage by creating the skills necessary to negotiate meaning and build upon what they already know.

This series is about building *real skills* that will work in the *real world*. It is based on cutting-edge research in neuroscience and psychology. Enjoy exploring the creation of these dynamic skills that will lead to the *deeper understanding* of English and beyond!

Robert S. Murphy, series author
Deeper Understanding Books

visit DeeperUnderstandingBooks.com for more details and free online tutorials!

NOTES:

Optimal Levels! **Fun** Flavor

Book 1

Modules	Themes	Optional
Module 1	Travel	Ecology
Module 2	Shopping	Dressing Up
Module 3	Movies	Live Music
Module 4	Cooking	Weddings
Module 5	Games	Golfing
Module 6	Driving Around	New Foods

Title Optimal Levels!: Fun Flavor Book 1
Level STUDENT CENTERED: High Beginner to Advanced. Great for universities!
ISBN 978-1451539745
Price ¥2,980 (Include TAX ¥3,129)
Designed for FUN English courses! Six modules designed to foster a deep understanding in: Travel, Shopping, Movies, Cooking, Games, and Driving Around.

Modules	Themes	Optional
Module 1	Sports	The Suitcase
Module 2	Music	Happy Shopping
Module 3	Fashion	Moving Pictures
Module 4	Night Life	The Chef
Module 5	Eating Out	Handheld Games
Module 6	Parks	The Convertible

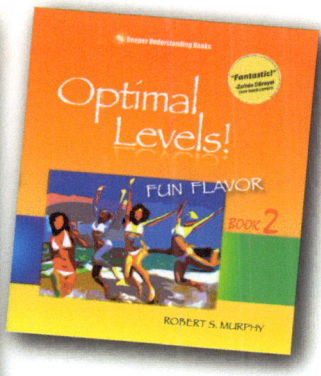

Book 2

Title Optimal Levels!: Fun Flavor Book 2
Level STUDENT CENTERED: High Beginner to Advanced. Great for universities!
ISBN 978-4905117018
Price ¥2,980 (Include TAX ¥3,129)
Students who complete the Fun flavor Book 1 deserve to move on to Book 2. Book two is designed to be more cognitively challenging than Book 1 and naturally provides a solid boost in students' performance. Topics covered in this Book 2 are: Sports, Music, Fashion, Night Life, Eating Out, and Parks. The topics in this book have been chosen to continue motivating young students through their English learning. By the end of Book 2, your students will gain strong confidence in their English skills and will be able to have discussions on a wide range of appealing topics. Works best when combined with Optimal Levels! Project Book 2.

Optimal Levels! Original Flavor

Book 1

Modules	Themes	Optional
Module 1	Family	What's Floating?
Module 2	Hobbies	On the Wall
Module 3	Food	Huge Sandwich
Module 4	Dream House	Poolside Baby
Module 5	Sickness	Jumping for Joy
Module 6	Restaurants	The Village

Title Optimal Levels!: Original Flavor Book 1
Level STUDENT CENTERED: High Beginner to Advanced.
ISBN 978-1451553284
Price ¥2,980 (Include TAX ¥3,129)
Designed for your standard English courses with mature students. Six modules designed to foster a deep understanding in: Family, Hobbies, Food, Dream House, Sickness, and Restaurants. Six topics chosen for mature students interested in a general English conversation. Perfect for standard eikaiwa classes. For younger (or younger at heart) students choose the FUN flavor. Works best when combined with Optimal Levels! Project Book.

Modules	Themes	Optional
Module 1	Dream House	The Family
Module 2	Medical Care	The Ball Game
Module 3	Restaurants	Pasta!
Module 4	Animals	Tropical House
Module 5	Religions	Fever?
Module 6	Friends	An Oyster Bar

Book 2

Title Optimal Levels!: Original Flavor Book 2
Level STUDENT CENTERED: High Beginner to Advanced. Great for universities!
ISBN 978-4905117025
Price ¥2,980 (Include TAX ¥3,129)
Students who complete the Original Flavor Book 1 deserve to move on to Book 2. Book two is designed to be more cognitively challenging than Book 1 and naturally provides a solid boost in student performance. Topics covered in this Book 2 are: Dream House, Medical Care, Restaurants, Animals, Religious, Friends. The first module eases the transition into Book 2 by returning to a popular topic from Book 1. By the end of Book 2, your students will have a strong foundation in conversational English. Works best when combined with Optimal Levels! Project Book 2.

Optimal Levels!  Medical Flavor

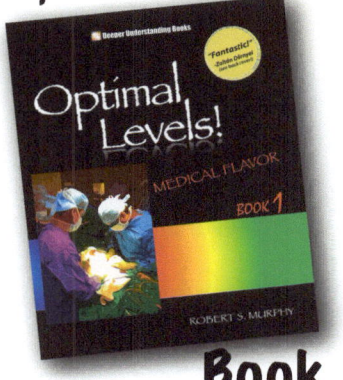

Book 1

Modules	Themes	Optional
Module 1	Hospital Room	Space Station
Module 2	Sickness	A Restaurant
Module 3	Care	Violin Music
Module 4	All about you!	The Singer
Module 5	Surgery	Retro Car
Module 6	Treatment	The Studio

Title Optimal Levels!: Medical Flavor Book 1
Level STUDENT CENTERED: High Beginner to Advanced. Great for medical students and nursing courses!
ISBN 978-1451551655
Price ¥2,980 (Include TAX ¥3,129)
Designed for MEDICAL English courses! Six modules designed to foster a deep understanding in: The Hospital Room, Sicknesses, Care, Personal Talk, Surgery, and Treatment. Six topics chosen for Medical students (doctors and nurses) or anyone interested in learning medical talk! Works best when combined with Optimal Levels! Project Book.

Modules	Themes	Optional
Module 1		
Module 2		
Module 3	Coming soon!	
Module 4		
Module 5		
Module 6		

Coming soon!

Book 2

Title Optimal Levels!: Medical Flavor Book 2
Level STUDENT CENTERED: High Beginner to Advanced.
ISBN
Price ¥2,980 (Include TAX ¥3,129)

Optimal Levels! Business Flavor

Book 1

Modules	Themes	Optional
Module 1	Money	Car on the Beach
Module 2	Presentations	The Waterfall
Module 3	Investing	Art Gallery
Module 4	Communication	The Great Hamburger
Module 5	Marketing	The Sneakers
Module 6	Management	Planes and Trains

Title Optimal Levels!: Business Flavor Book 1
Level STUDENT CENTERED: High Beginner to Advanced. Great for Business students!
ISBN 978-1451555165
Price ¥2,980 (Include TAX ¥3,129)
Designed for BUSINESS English courses! Six modules designed to foster a deep understanding in: Money, Presentations, Investing, Communication, Marketing, and Management. Six topics chosen for Business students or anyone interesting in learning to talk business! Works best when combined with Optimal Levels! Project Book.

Modules	Themes	Optional
Module 1	Leadership	Money
Module 2	Contracts	Presentations
Module 3	Negotiations	Investing
Module 4	Global Marketing	Communication
Module 5	Office Troubles	Marketing
Module 6	Networks	Management

Book 2

Title Optimal Levels!: Business Flavor Book 2
Level STUDENT CENTERED: High Beginner to Advanced. Great for Business students!
ISBN 978-4905117032
Price ¥2,980 (Include TAX ¥3,129)
Students who complete Business flavor Book 1 deserve to move on to Book 2. Book two is designed to be more cognitively challenging than Book 1 and naturally provides a solid boost in student performance.
Topics covered in this Book 2 are: Leadership, Contracts, Negotiations, Global Marketing, Office Troubles, and Networks. By the end of Book 2, your students will have a fantastic foundation in Business English that they will be proud of. You'll be proud of them, too! Works best when combined with Optimal Levels! Project Book 2.

Optimal Levels! Philosophy Flavor

Modules	Themes	Optional
Module 1	Love	The Blossom
Module 2	Justice	Guilty
Module 3	Humanity	Evolution
Module 4	Economy	Manhattan
Module 5	Art	The Jazz Bar
Module 6	Freedom	On the Wings...

Book 1

Title Optimal Levels!: Philosophy Flavor Book 1
Level STUDENT CENTERED: High Beginner to Advanced. Very popular at universities!
ISBN 978-1451553284
Price ¥2,980 (Include TAX ¥3,129)

Philosophy in English class? Yes! Enjoy watching your students grow with great themes from Philosophy. These six modules are designed to foster a deep understanding in: Love, Justice, Humanity, Economy, Art, and Freedom. Teachers and student have great fun with this *Philosophy Flavor*. Very popular at universities! Works best when combined with *Optimal Levels! Project Book*.

Modules	Themes	Optional
Module 1	Happiness	The Couple
Module 2	Religion	What is Fair?
Module 3	War	Humanity
Module 4	Education	Getting Paid
Module 5	Democracy	Artistic Freedom
Module 6	Communism	In Chains?

Book 2

Title Optimal Levels!: Philosophy Flavor Book 2
Level Beginner STUDENT CENTERED: High Beginner to Advanced. Very popular at universities!
ISBN
Price ¥2,980 (Include TAX ¥3,129)

Students hungry for more Philosophy? Book 2 is the answer! Enjoy watching your students grow even further with these big themes from Philosophy. These six modules are designed to foster a deep understanding in: Happiness, Religion, War, Education, Democracy, and Communism. Heavy topics for your best students! Very popular at universities! Works best when combined with *Optimal Levels! Project Book*.

Optimal Levels! PROJECT BOOKS

Book 1

Title Optimal Levels! Project Book (1)
Level High Beginner to Advanced. Works well with any textbook!
ISBN 978-1451557893

Price ¥2,500 （Include TAX ¥2,625）
Designed for any 'flavor' of Optimal Levels!, or any course that requires deeper understanding and presentation assistance! Optimal Levels! PROJECT BOOK provides students with a wide variety of project choices of differing levels -some are writing intensive, some are drawing intensive, while others are purely 'thinking' intensive. All the projects are designed to help the students culminate their learning into class presentations that can be assessed peer-to-peer and/or by the teacher. Works very well with mixed classes and differentiated instruction too! Optimal Levels is an exciting new textbook series for English, ESL, and EFL classrooms. These textbooks have been designed to maximize student thinking and the construction of cognitive skills through the usage of the English language. This series is based upon the author's research in Mind, Brain, and Education at Harvard University and research in TEFL/TESL at the University of Birmingham. Rather than presenting to students what must be learned, this series proposes motivating themes and scaffolded tasks that are designed to build skills dynamically. By doing the theme-based student-centered tasks, students dynamically learn and understand language usage by creating the skills necessary to negotiate meaning and build upon what they already know. Highly motivational and highly effective!

Title Optimal Levels! Project Book 2 : The perfect companion to your Textbook!
Level High Beginner to Advanced. Works well with any textbook!
ISBN 978-4905117001

Price Price ¥2,500 （Include TAX ¥2,625）
Project Book 2 has a strong focus on paragraph writing, five paragraph essay writing, and presentation designing. Choose this Project Book if you want to raise academic writing *and* presentation skills for any subject! This project books are very popular among students and teachers -especially in classes where essay writing is essential! By doing the theme-based student-centered tasks, students dynamically learn and understand language usage by creating the skills necessary to negotiate meaning and build upon what they already know. The projects are designed to take them through cognitive processing needed to plan and write effective essays *and* fantastic presentations. Highly motivational and highly effective!

Book 2

EXCERPT from PROJECT BOOK 2

How to use this book (it's all about building skills!)

This PROJECT BOOK has been designed to be the ultimate companion for any of the "flavors" in the **Optimal Levels!** textbook series or any course that requires deeper understanding or presentation help.

How many projects per module (unit) of study?

All of the projects in this book have been designed to foster deeper understanding.

For classes that meet daily: doing each project in this book should prove to be wonderfully effective, but doing all of them is certainly not necessary. Allow students to make their own project choices.

For classes that meet only once or twice a week: allow students to choose one or two projects from A-D (as warm ups), then go on to the paragraph and presentation development projects. These projects can be done during class time and/or done for homework. Make sure the students understand that these projects are (a) designed to help them gain a deeper understanding of the material, and (b) designed to help them build well founded ideas for their class presentations.

The class presentation?

The presentation is the culmination of all the work than went into the module!

Assessment of these presentations is typically more reliable than memorization-based paper tests. Allow the students to do peer-to-peer assessment as a strategy to (a) raise their own awareness of the content and (b) raise their awareness of presentation skills. Through the affects of this ongoing assessment, by the end of the book, most students should show significant improvement across the board. Allow students to choose their own presentation topic per module within the general theme of the current module.

Students can use the "MY PRESENTATION" pages to design their paper-based presentations. On the day of the presentations, students in small classes can show what they have drawn on these six pages to their peers during their presentations. For larger classes the pages may be scanned and/or projected overhead as typical computer-based presentations are done.

Student (peer-to-peer) assessment?

The metacognition that goes on during peer-to-peer assessment is highly desirable because it helps build crucial strategic networks in the brain. Allow the students to decide the best assessment criteria (perhaps from a list of ideas that you can provide such as: *pronunciation, vocabulary usage, grammar, voice, fluency, eye-contact, charisma, etc.*) Allowing students to 'sanction' the assessment criteria is often a motivation booster. This motivation helps students stay focused on their goals which in turn drives them to higher performance.

Have students choose up to three assessment areas and write them in spaces A, B, and C at the top of the page. Grading is simple. Students circle the appropriate level (1 is lowest and 5 is highest, just as in the main textbooks) based on their own best judgement.

For some students, simply circling numbers may become tedious. Allowing students to choose the 'top three', and/or write some sort of comment in the spaces on the right side may prove to be a big attention-getter and will undoubtably help foster further metacognition.

"Tri-elemental"? What is "Teaching for the DATC"?

Language acquisition can be depicted as being tri-elemental: *Linguistic Structures, Socio-cultural Manifestations,* and *Non-verbal(emotional) Manifestations*. These three are context-dependent and grow dynamically. Naturally, the convergence area of these three elements also grows dynamically. Too much focus on Linguistic Structures and not enough focus on Culture and/or Non-verbal manifestations creates an unbalanced language learning context. Strive for a balanced DATC!

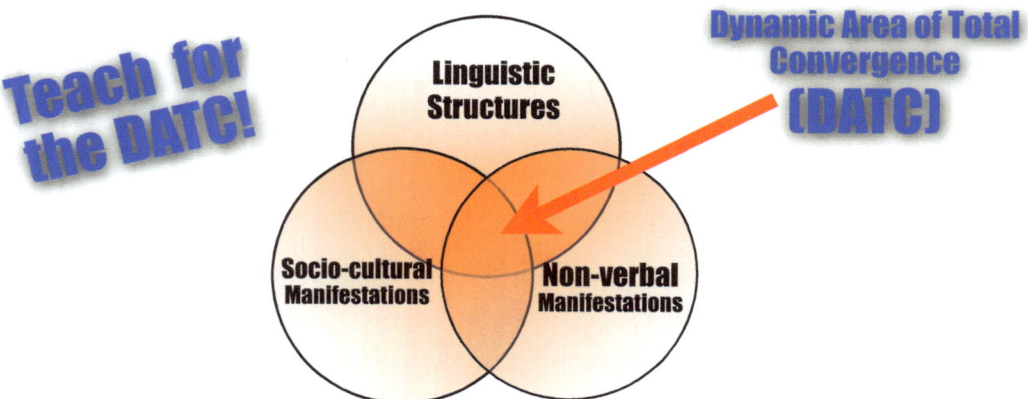

The entire Optimal Levels! series is written in a "Teaching for the DATC" format!

Neuroscientific Design!

Optimal Levels!

Book 1 Series
Sample pages and tutorials

Section 1. Introduction

Look at the picture above. Ask and answer "who, what, when, where, why, how" questions.

Your questions	Your answers	Partner's answers
Q1. What do you see?		
Q2. _____		
Q3. _____		
Q4. _____		

Feelings/emotions from the picture:

_ _ _ _ _ _ _ _ _ _

Performance of Understanding Time!

Discussion:
"This picture makes me feel..."

Section 2. Word map to expression!

 Choose your own Root Word from the picture in Section 1 and create a word map.

$\oplus$ positive
$\ominus$ negative

Write three sentences from your word map ideas!
Draw pictures!

Sentence A

Picture A

Sentence B

Picture B

Sentence C

Picture C

low   high
Self-assessment of sentences: 1 2 3 4 5

15

Section 3. Expansion

Work with a partner. Write your partner's sentences below. Discuss.

Partner's Sentence A

Partner's Sentence B

Partner's Sentence C

low   high
Give your partner a score! 1 2 3 4 5

Performance of Understanding Time!

Discuss how the Root Word connects to culture and society. Write in the chart below.
Receive a Deep Understanding Score from your partner.

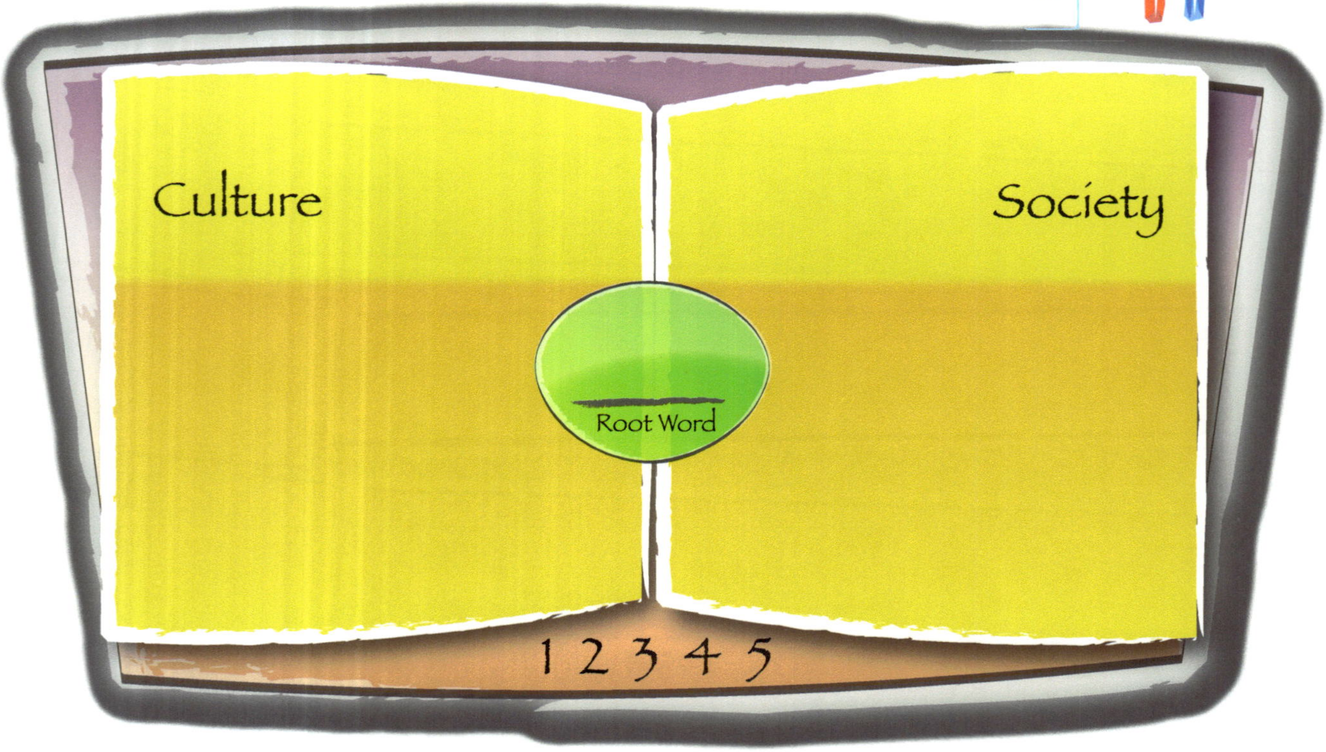

Culture   Society

Root Word

1 2 3 4 5

Section 4. Lexical Analysis!

Find coordinates, collocations, synonyms, and hyponyms of the Root Word. Write them on the cards.

A Coordinates with Root Word
salt - pepper - ketchup - mustard

B Collocations of Root Word
big house, birds fly, spicy curry

Root Word

hot-spicy, lost-missing, tall-high
C Synonyms of Root Word

COLOR(red, blue), MONEY(yen, euro)
D Hyponyms of Root Word

low   high
Self-assessment: 1 2 3 4 5

Section 5. Lexical Performance Time!

Write sentences using the connections you made in Section 4.

A Sentence using "coordinates" of Root Word

My score for this sentence: 1 2 3 4 5

B Sentence using "collocation" of Root Word

My score for this sentence: 1 2 3 4 5

C Sentence using "synonym" of Root Word

My score for this sentence: 1 2 3 4 5

D Sentence using "hyponym" of Root Word

My score for this sentence: 1 2 3 4 5

Exchange your book with your partner.
Discuss your sentences. Make corrections if necessary.
Give yourself a final score for each sentence.

Section 6. High Performance!

Write a short story using your ideas from this module.

Title:

Date:

Feelings/Emotions discussed:

Socio-culture discussed:

Deep Understanding Scores:

shallow   deep   shallow   deep
1 2 3 4 5   1 2 3 4 5
Partner   Teacher

Fill in the box above.
Discuss. Receive scores and advice from your partner and teacher!

Section 7. Final Performance of Understanding!

Make your story even better!

Title

Date

Receive scores from your partner and teacher:

shallow   deep   shallow   deep
1 2 3 4 5   1 2 3 4 5
Partner   Teacher

Was your partner helpful?
Score your partner's help level: [1 2 3 4 5]

IMAGINATION EXPRESS

Look carefully at the picture above. Think of matching adverbs and adjectives.
Write them down. Make sentences.

Adverbs for this picture.	Adjectives for this picture.

shallow   deep
Score: 1 2 3 4 5

THINK AGAIN

Think about the unit you just finished. Answer these questions.

1. What did you enjoy about this unit?

2. How can you connect what you learned to the real world?

3. What have you become interested in because of this unit?

4. Ideas for improving your skills:

low   high
Self-assessment: 1 2 3 4 5

Tutorial for Book 1 (it's all about building skills!)

Teachers, adjust the following instructions to match your students' levels.
FREE ONLINE TUTORIALS too!
DeeperUnderstandingBooks.com

Section 1. Introduction

Look carefully at the provided picture. This picture represents the theme for this entire unit. What questions can you come up with? Think and then write down three more *"who, what, when, where, why, and how"* questions. After you have written the questions in the boxes, think of answers to your own questions and write them down too. Find a partner. Ask your questions to your partner and then write your partner's answers in the boxes next to your own answers. *How different were your answers?*

Feelings/emotions from the picture: Write down one or two feelings/emotions that you get from the picture.

Performance of Understanding Time! Find a partner. Discuss how the picture makes you feel and why. Compare answers with your partner. *How different were your answers?* Discuss with your teacher!

Section 1. Introduction

Look at the picture above. Ask and answer "who, what, when, where, why, how" questions.

Your questions	Your answers	Partner's answers
Q1. What do you see?		
Q2. _____		
Q3. _____		
Q4. _____		

Performance of Understanding Time!

Discussion:
"This picture makes me *feel…*"

from Philosophy Flavor Book 1

Section 2. Word map to expression!

Choose your own Root Word from the picture in Section 1 and create a word map.

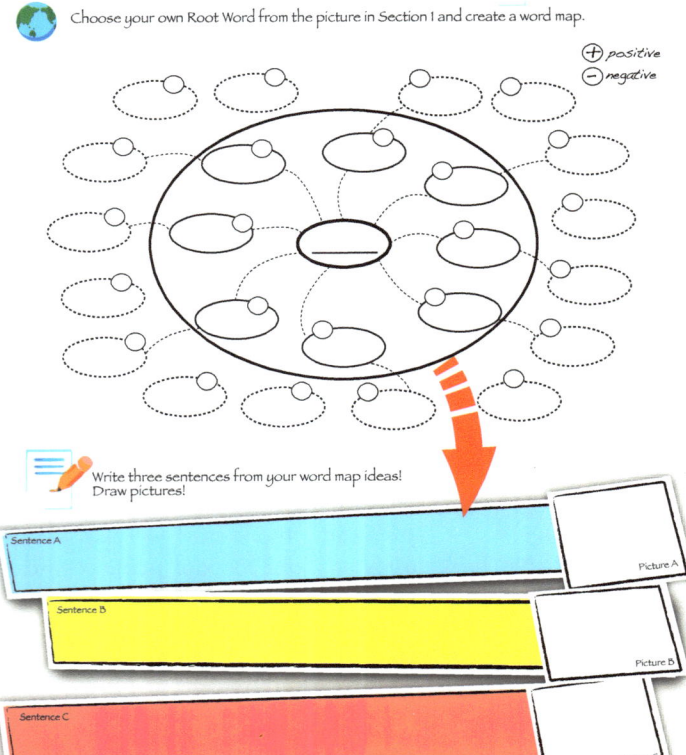

⊕ positive
⊖ negative

Write three sentences from your word map ideas!
Draw pictures!

Sentence A

Picture A

Sentence B

Picture B

Sentence C

Picture C

Self-assessment of sentences: 1 2 3 4 5

Section 2. Word map to expression!

Choose one word (or one phrase) as the *Root Word* for the word map. The Root Word can be anything that you think matches this module's theme. Write the Root Word in the middle of the word map. Use your imagination and connect as many first generation links to other words as possible. Decide if the connections are positive or negative. Write a *plus (+)* or a *minus (-)* mark in the small circles. Next, use your imagination and create second generation connections. Write a *plus (+)* or a *minus (-)* mark in the small circles. There are eight 'floating connections'. Use these as you wish. You can make them first, second, or even third generation connections.

Write three sentences... Look carefully at your completed word map. You can probably think of many sentences. Write down three good sentences: Sentence A, Sentence B, and Sentence C. Next, draw one picture about each sentence next to each sentence.

Self-assessment of sentences: Think about your sentences. Choose what you want to assess about them. (Are they well connected to the theme? Do your sentences make sense? Are they grammatically correct?) *Did you do well?* Give yourself a score! [Scoring: 1 is low and 5 is high.]

Section 3. Expansion

Find a partner. Ask your partner to dictate his/her three sentences to you. Write them down in the boxes. Think about your partner's sentences. Choose what you want to assess about them. (Are they well connected to the theme? Do the sentences make sense? Are they grammatically correct?) Give your partner a score! [Scoring: 1 is low and 5 is high.]

Performance of Understanding Time! Find a partner. Discuss your Root Words and how they connect to *culture (old culture and new/pop culture).* Write your ideas down. Next, discuss how your Root Words connect to *society (any society).* Write your ideas down. When you are finished, look at your partner's book. *How deep are your partner's ideas?* Give your partner a Deep Understanding Score (and receive a score from your partner). Discuss your ideas with your teacher.

Section 3. Expansion

Work with a partner. Write your partner's sentences below. Discuss.

Partner's Sentence A

Partner's Sentence B

Partner's Sentence C

low high
Give your partner a score! 1 2 3 4 5

Performance of Understanding Time!

Discuss how the Root Word connects to culture and society. Write in the chart below. Receive a Deep Understanding Score from your partner.

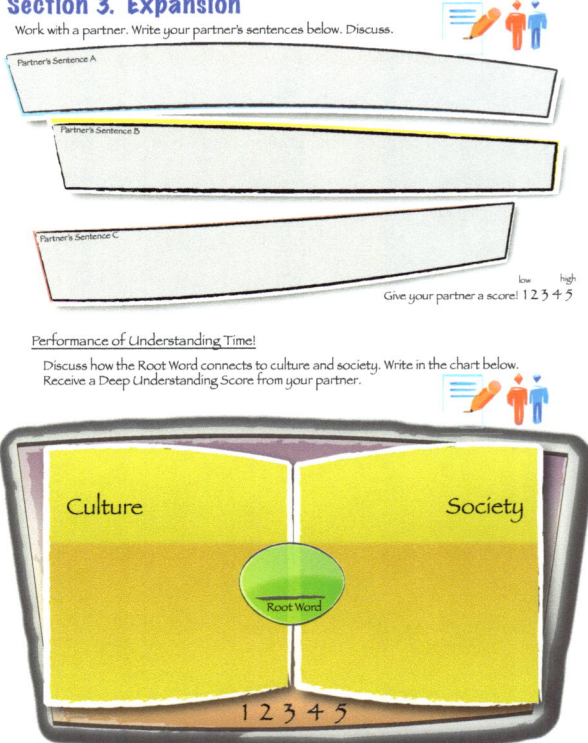

Section 4. Lexical Analysis!

Find coordinates, collocations, synonyms, and hyponyms of the Root Word. Write them on the cards.

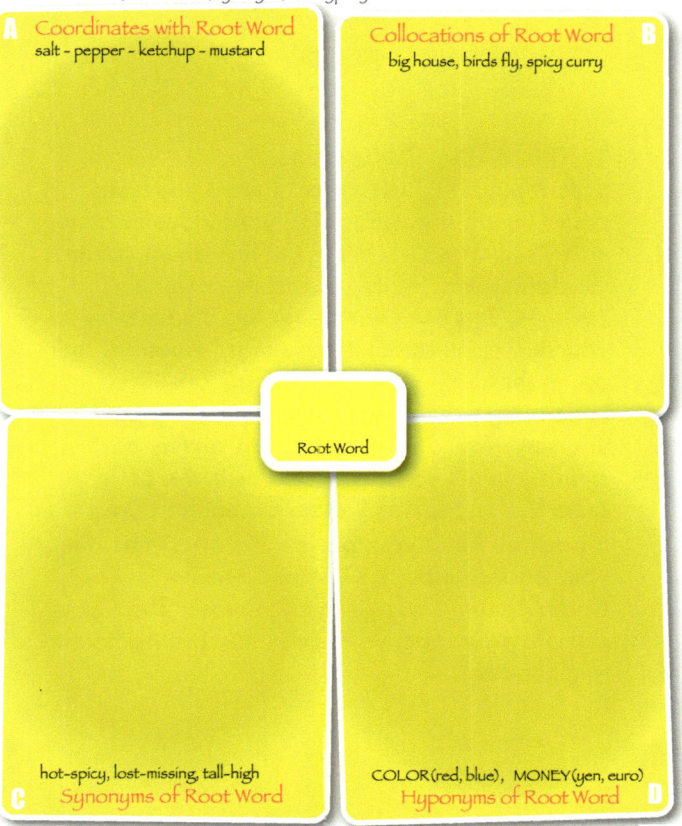

A Coordinates with Root Word
salt - pepper - ketchup - mustard

B Collocations of Root Word
big house, birds fly, spicy curry

Root Word

C hot-spicy, lost-missing, tall-high
Synonyms of Root Word

D COLOR (red, blue), MONEY (yen, euro)
Hyponyms of Root Word

low   high
Self-assessment: 1 2 3 4 5

Section 4. Lexical Analysis

Write your Root Word in the Root Word box in the center of the page.

Card A: Coordinates Write down *coordinates* for the Root Word. Coordinates are words that are in the same general group, on the same level, and have a similar function. A good example is: "salt - pepper - ketchup - mustard".

Card B: Collocations Write down *collocations* for the Root Word. Collocations are words that fit next to the Root Word. Good example are: "*big* house", "*red* house", "*expensive* house" and "house *guest*".

Card C: Synonyms Write down *synonyms* for the Root Word. Synonyms are words that have the same or a similar meaning. Good examples are: "hot - *spicy*", "hot - *boiling*", and "hot - *sexy*".

Card D: Hyponyms Write down *hyponyms* for the Root Word. Hyponyms are words that belong to a set of words descriptive of, but are "*below*", the root word. Good examples are "Color (*red, blue, green*)", "Money (*dollars, yen, euro*)", and "Computer (*CPU, RAM, HDD*)"   (If you cannot think of hyponyms, you can use *hypernyms* - words that are "above" the Root Word. Color is a hypernym of red.)

Self-assessment: Choose what you want to assess. How well did you do? Give yourself a self-assessment (1 to 5).

Section 5. Lexical Performance Time!

Card A: Coordinates Write down a sentence using *coordinates* for the Root Word. A good example is: "I like to put *salt* and *pepper* on steak, but a hot dog needs *ketchup* and *mustard!*"

Card B: Collocations Write down a sentence using *collocations* for the Root Word. A good example is "Today I live in a *small* house, but some day I want to live in a *big* house!"

Card C: Synonyms Write down a sentence using *synonyms* for the Root Word. A good example is "I thought the Indian curry would be very *hot*, but it was not as *spicy* as I had expected!"

Card D: Hyponyms Write down a sentence using *hyponyms* for the Root Word. A good example is "I bought a new set of cutlery - *forks, knives, and spoons!*"

Exchange your book... Find a partner. Exchange your book with your partner. Discuss your sentences. Ask questions. Are there any mistakes? Correct the mistakes that you find. Return your partner's book.

Self-assessment: Choose what you want to assess. How well did you do? Give yourself a self-assessment for each sentence (1 to 5).

Section 5. Lexical Performance Time!

Write sentences using the connections you made in Section 4.

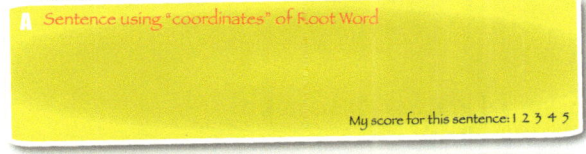

A Sentence using "coordinates" of Root Word

My score for this sentence: 1 2 3 4 5

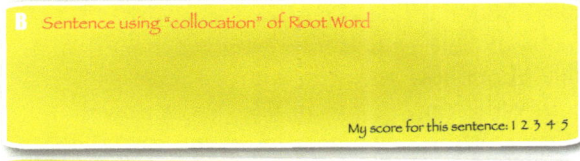

B Sentence using "collocation" of Root Word

My score for this sentence: 1 2 3 4 5

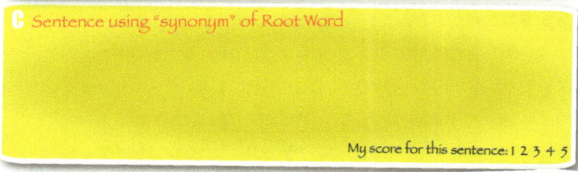

C Sentence using "synonym" of Root Word

My score for this sentence: 1 2 3 4 5

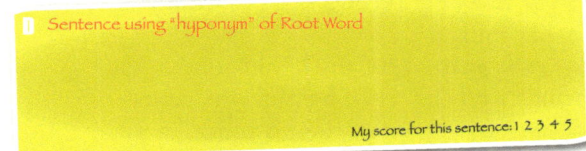

D Sentence using "hyponym" of Root Word

My score for this sentence: 1 2 3 4 5

Exchange your book with your partner.
Discuss your sentences. Make corrections if necessary.
Give yourself a final score for each sentence.

Section 6. High Performance!

Write a short story using your ideas from this module.

Title:

Date:

Feelings/Emotions discussed:

Socio-culture discussed:

Deep Understanding Scores:

shallow   deep   shallow   deep

1 2 3 4 5   1 2 3 4 5

Partner   Teacher

Fill in the box above.
Discuss. Receive scores and advice from your partner and teacher!

Section 6. High Performance!

Look though the unit. Look at what you have done. Imagine a story using your ideas from this unit. Think of a title. Write the title down. Write the date down. Write your story down!

Feelings/Emotions discussed: Read your story to yourself. Think about the feelings/ emotions that are in the story. Write them in the box.

Socio-culture discussed: Read your story to yourself. *How does it connect to society and culture?* Write your a few words in the box.

Deep Understanding Scores: Exchange books with a partner. Read your partner's story. Think about your partner's story. Give and receive *Deep Understanding Scores* to each other. Show your story to your teacher. Receive a score from your teacher, too!

Section 7. Final Performance of Understanding!

Make your story even better!

Title

Date

Receive scores from your partner and teacher:

shallow   deep   shallow   deep

1 2 3 4 5   1 2 3 4 5

Partner   Teacher

Was your partner helpful?
Score your partner's help level: [1 2 3 4 5]

Section 7. Final Performance of Understanding!

Think about the scores that you received from your partner and from your teacher. Think about how your can improve your story. Write down a newer title. Write down the date. Write down your improved story!

Deep Understanding Scores: Exchange books with a partner. Read your partner's new story. Think about your partner's story. Give and receive new *Deep Understanding Scores* to each other. Show your new story to your teacher. Receive a score from your teacher too!

Was your partner helpful? Think about your partner's advice. How helpful was your partner? Give your partner a score (in your own book -you don't have to show your partner this score.)

IMAGINATION EXPRESS

Look carefully at the picture above. Think of matching adverbs and adjectives.
Write them down. Make sentences.

Adverbs for this picture.	Adjectives for this picture.

shallow   deep
Score: 1 2 3 4 5

OPTIONAL: IMAGINATION EXPRESS

Look carefully at the picture. What do you see?

Adverbs: *Which adverbs match the picture?* Write them in the box.

Adverbs: *Which adjectives match the picture?* Write them in the box.

Use your adverbs and adjectives to make interesting sentences about the picture.

Deep Understanding Score: Read your sentences to yourself. Think about your sentences. Give yourself a *Deep Understanding Score.*

19

THINK AGAIN

Think about the unit you just finished. Answer these questions.

1. What did you enjoy about this unit?

2. How can you connect what you learned to the real world?

3. What have you become interested in because of this unit?

4. Ideas for improving your skills:

low   high
Self-assessment: 1 2 3 4 5

OPTIONAL: THINK AGAIN

Think about what you have accomplished during this unit. Answer the four questions. Take your time. (Write good, well-developed answers to the questions.) Use these answers to help your future studies.

Book 2 Series
Sample pages and tutorials

Friends

6

Section 1. Introduction

Look at the picture above. Ask and answer "who, what, when, where, why, how" questions.

Your questions	Your answers	Partner's answers
Q1. What do you see?		
Q2. ____		
Q3. ____		
Q4. ____		

Feelings/emotions from the picture:

------------------.

Performance of Understanding Time!

Discussion:
"This picture makes me feel…"

Section 2. Word map to expression!

 Choose your own Root Word from the picture in Section 1 and create a word map.

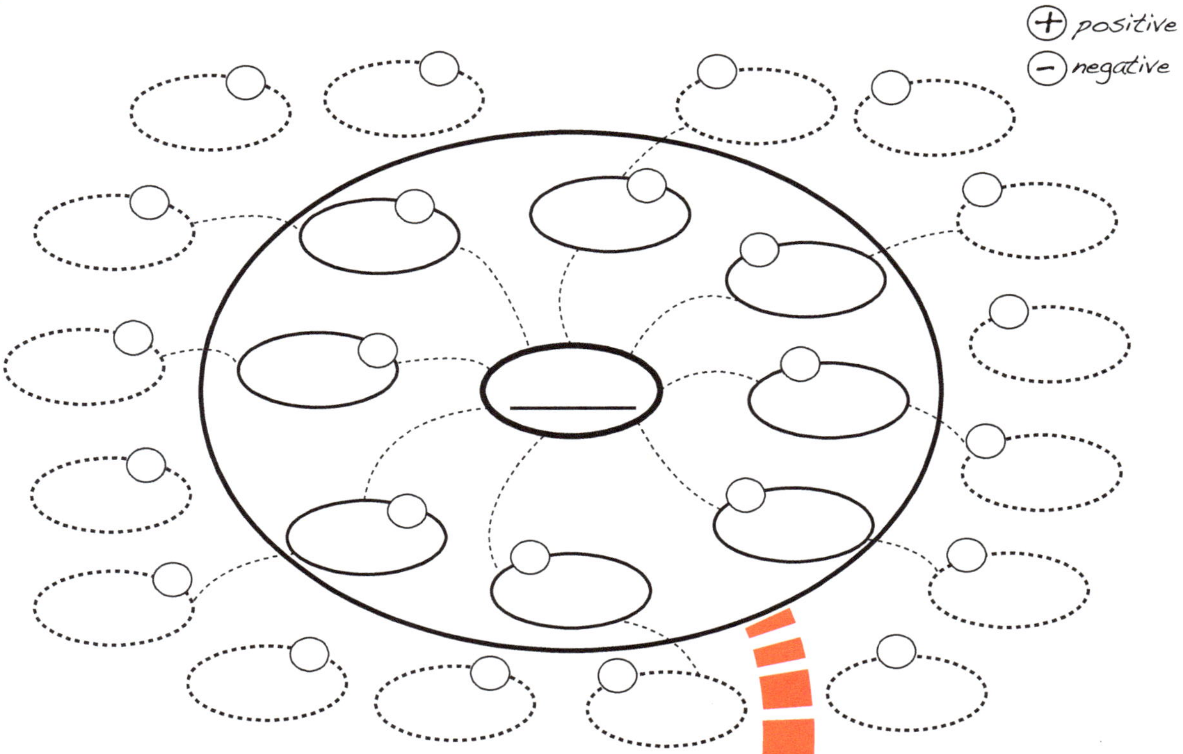

$\bigoplus$ positive
$\bigominus$ negative

Find three main ideas from your word map!
Write them in the boxes below.

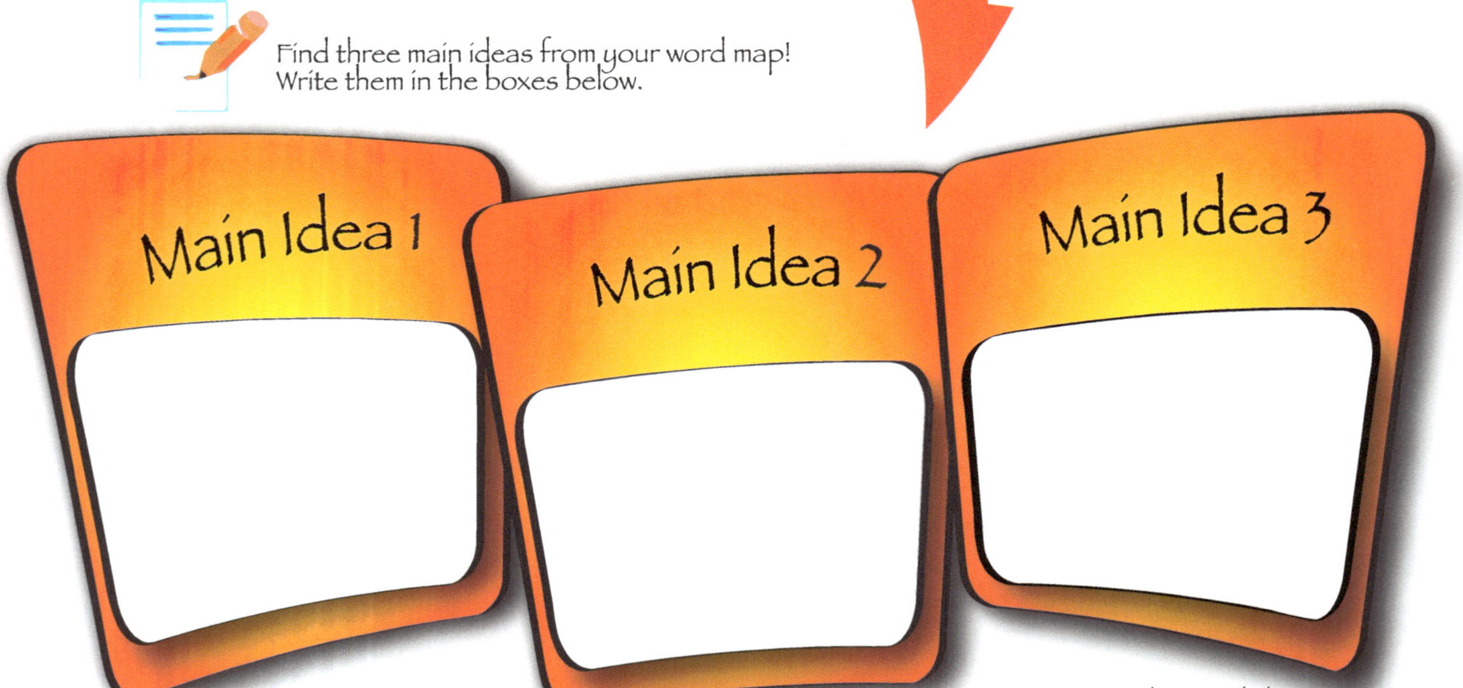

Main Idea 1

Main Idea 2

Main Idea 3

Self-assessment of ideas: low 1 2 3 4 5 high

Section 3. Expansion

Think about your three Main Ideas. Write them below. Also write down the Linguistic, Socio-cultural, and Feelings/Emotional connections you find.

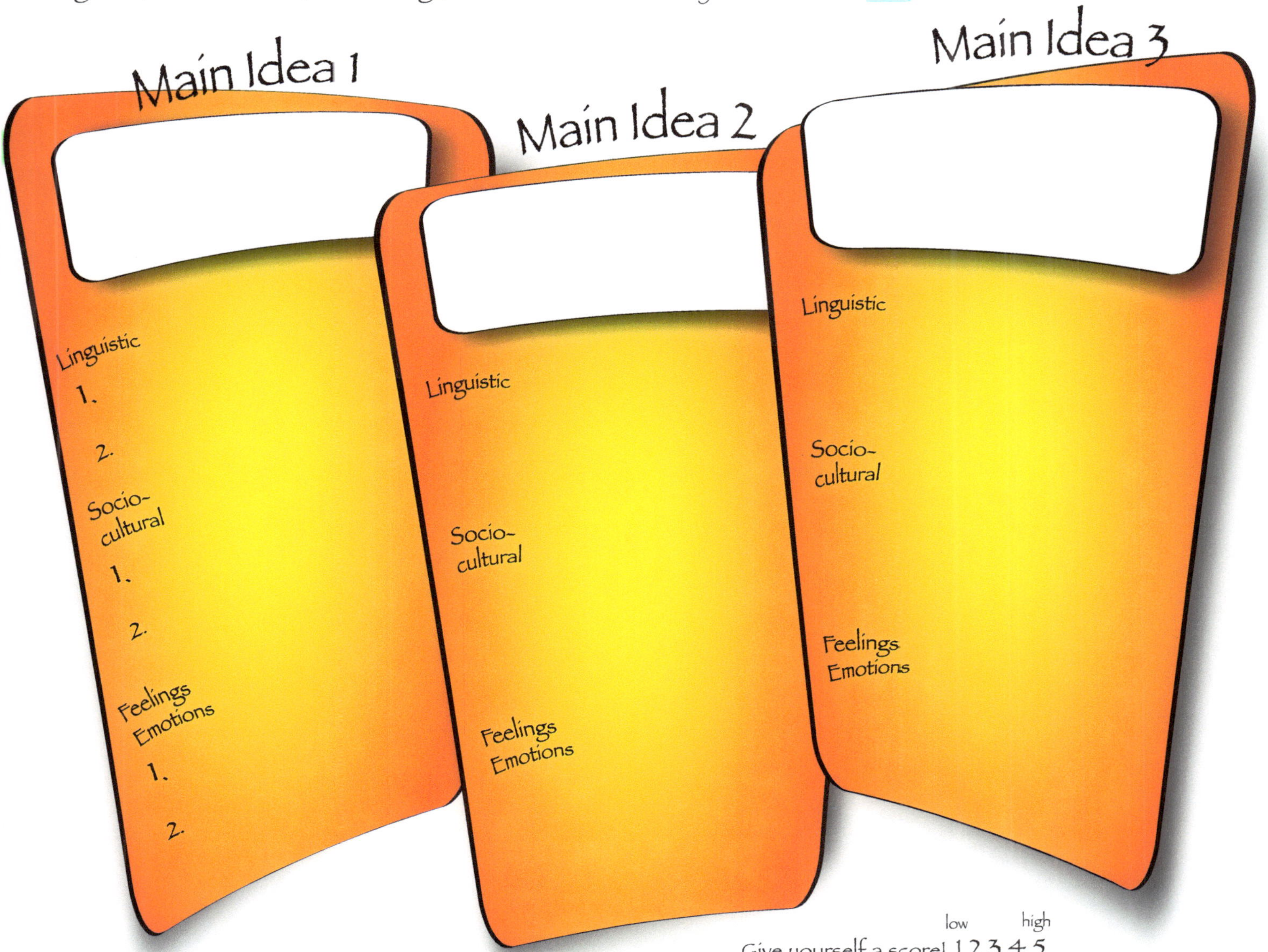

Main Idea 1

Linguistic

1.

2.

Socio-cultural

1.

2.

Feelings Emotions

1.

2.

Main Idea 2

Linguistic

Socio-cultural

Feelings Emotions

Main Idea 3

Linguistic

Socio-cultural

Feelings Emotions

low   high
Give yourself a score! 1 2 3 4 5

DRAW CONNECTIONS

Blue/black for positive connections
Red for negative connections

31

Section 4. Connection Analysis!

Find six connections from Section 3. Write them down in the boxes below. Explain the connections.

Explain the connection!

1. Connection!

2. Connection!

3. Connection!

4. Connection!

5. Connection!

6. Connection!

low   high

Self-assessment: 1 2 3 4 5

Section 5. Partner's Connections!

Ask you partner about his/her connections. Write them down in the boxes below.

Explain the connection!

1.
Connection!

2.
Connection!

3.
Connection!

4.
Connection!

5.
Connection!

6.
Connection!

low   high
Partner assessment: 1 2 3 4 5

Section 6. Paragraph Writing!

Write paragraphs using your connections! Draw pictures too! Get advice.

Picture!

Connection!

Picture!

Connection!

low   high
Partner's assessment: 1 2 3 4 5
Teacher's assessment: 1 2 3 4 5

Section 7. Better Paragraphs!

Make your paragraphs even better!

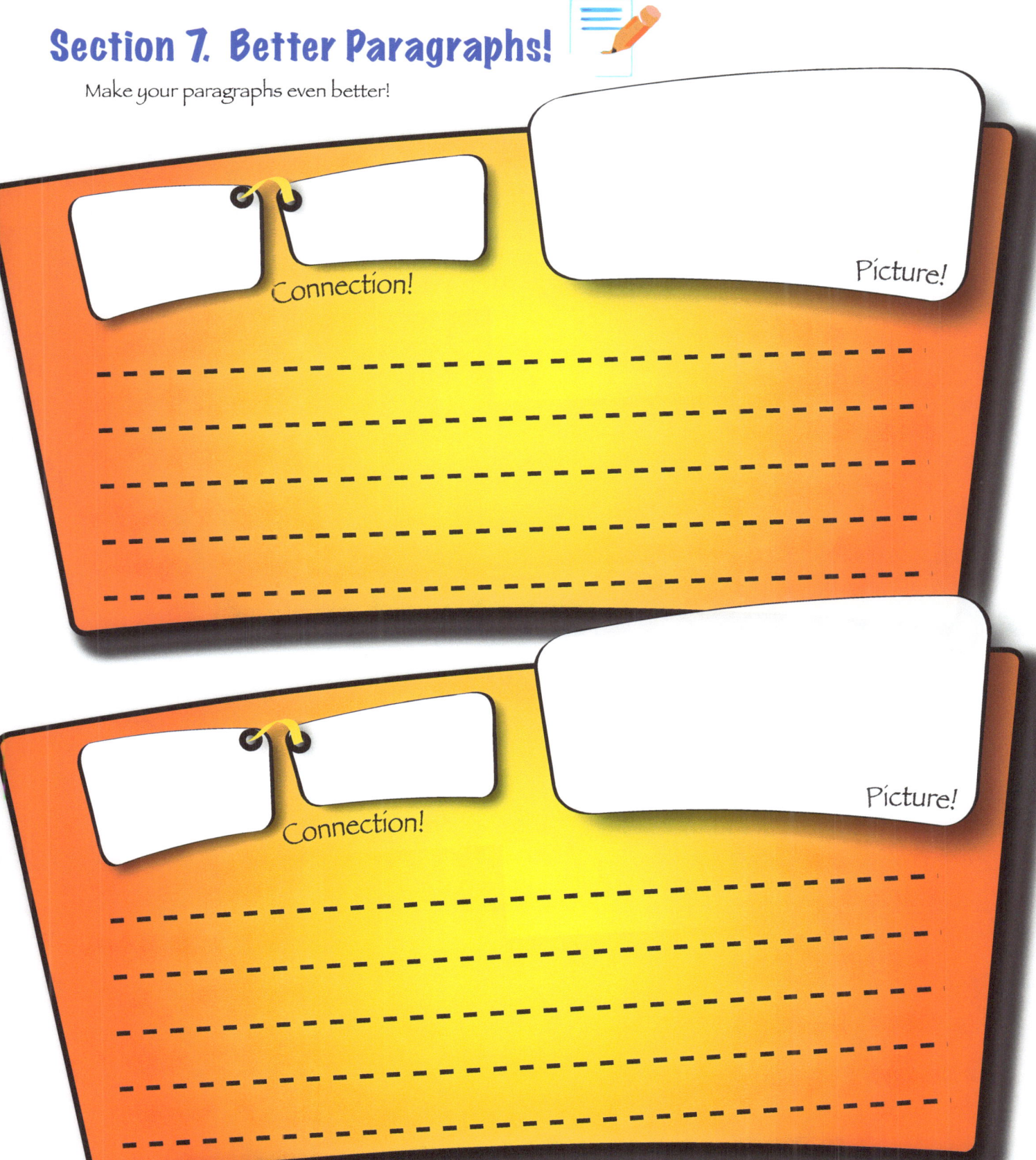

Connection!

Picture!

Connection!

Picture!

Was your partner helpful?
Score your partner's help level: [1 2 3 4 5]

low   high
Teacher's assessment: 1 2 3 4 5

IMAGINATION EXPRESS

Look carefully at the picture above. Think of matching adverbs and adjectives.
Write them down. Make sentences.

Adverbs for this picture.

Adjectives for this picture.

shallow   deep
Score: 1 2 3 4 5

THINK AGAIN

Think about the unit you just finished. Answer these questions.

1. What did you enjoy about this unit?

2. How can you connect what you learned to the real world?

3. What have you become interested in because of this unit?

4. Ideas for improving your skills:

low   high

Self-assessment: 1 2 3 4 5

Tutorial for BOOK 2 (it's all about building skills!)

Teachers, adjust the following instructions to match your students' levels.
FREE TUTORIALS! Visit DeeperUnderstandingBooks.com

Section 1. Introduction

Look at the picture above. Ask and answer "who, what, when, where, why, how" questions.

Your questions	Your answers	Partner's answers
Q1. What do you see?		
Q2. _____		
Q3. _____		
Q4. _____		

Section 1. Introduction
Look carefully at the provided picture. This picture represents the theme for this entire unit. What questions can you come up with? Think and then write down three more "who, what, when, where, why, and how" questions. After you have written the questions in the boxes, think of answers to your own questions and write them down too. Find a partner. Ask your questions to your partner and then write your partner's answers in the boxes next to your own answers. *How different were your answers?*

Feelings/emotions from the picture: Write down one or two feelings/emotions that you get from the picture.

Performance of Understanding Time! Find a partner. Discuss how the picture makes you feel and why. Compare answers with your partner. *How different were your answers?* Discuss with your teacher!

Feelings/emotions from the picture:

Performance of Understanding Time!

Discussion:
"This picture makes me *feel...*"

from Original Flavor Book 2

Choose your own Root Word from the picture in Section 1 and create a word map.

⊕ positive
⊖ negative

Find three main ideas from your word map. Write them in the boxes below.

Main Idea 1

Main Idea 2

Main Idea 3

Self-assessment of ideas: 1 2 3 4 5

58

Section 2. Word map to expression!

Choose one word (or one phrase) as the *Root Word* for the word map. The Root Word can be anything that you think matches this module's theme. Write the Root Word in the middle of the word map. Use your imagination and connect as many first generation links to other words as possible. Decide if the connections are positive or negative. Write a *plus (+)* or a *minus (-)* mark in the small circles. Next, use your imagination and create second generation connections. Write a *plus (+)* or a *minus (-)* mark in the small circles. There are eight 'floating connections'. Use these as you wish. You can make them first, second, or even third generation connections.

Find three Main Ideas... Look carefully at your completed word map. *Do you see any patterns? Do you see some common ideas?* Think carefully and write down three Main Ideas that strongly connect to the Root Word.

Self-assessment of sentences: Think about your work in Section 2. *Did you do well?* Give yourself a score! [Scoring: 1 is low and 5 is high.]

Section 3. Expansion

Think about your three Main Ideas. Write them below. Also write down the Linguistic, Socio-cultural, and Feelings/Emotional connections you find.

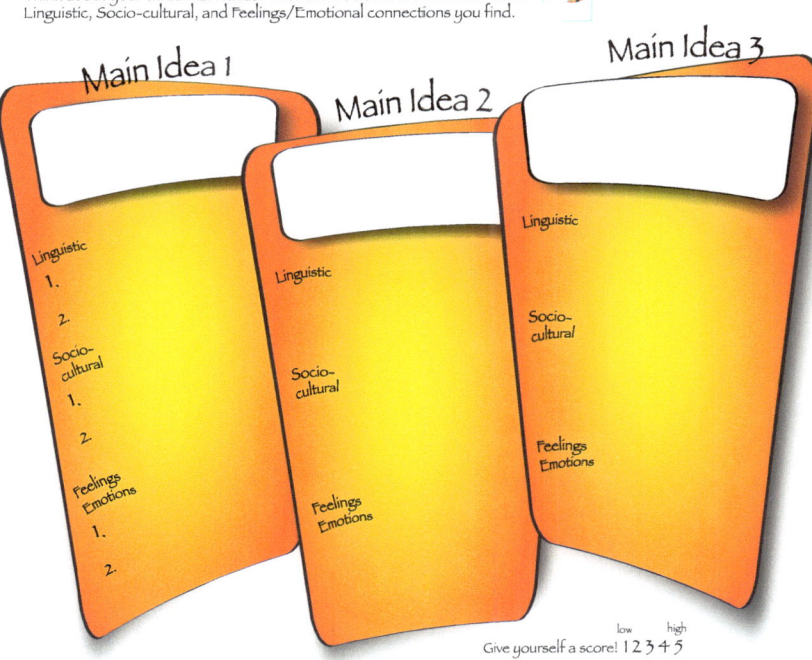

Main Idea 1

Main Idea 2

Main Idea 3

Linguistic
1.
2.
Socio-cultural
1.
2.
Feelings Emotions
1.
2.

Linguistic

Socio-cultural

Feelings Emotions

Linguistic

Socio-cultural

Feelings Emotions

low   high
Give yourself a score! 1 2 3 4 5

Section 3. Expansion

Write your three Main Ideas in the white boxes. Find at least two linguistic, socio- cultural, and feelings/emotional connections per Main Idea. Write them down. Choose what you want to assess about them. (*Are they well connected to the theme? Do they sentences make sense?*) Give your partner a score! [Scoring: 1 is low and 5 is high.]

DRAW CONNECTIONS Look carefully at your Main Ideas. *Can you draw connections between the words?* Use blue (or black) lines to draw positive connections. Use red for negative connections. Don't worry! There are no "right" or "wrong" answers here. Do you best in making new and interesting connections. Have fun with this! This activity will really expand your mind and make you think about this topic deeper than before.

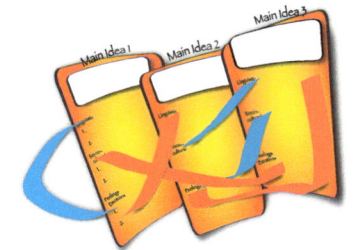

DRAW CONNECTIONS

Blue/black for positive connections
Red for negative connections!

Section 4. Connection Analysis!

Find six connections from Section 3. Write them down in the boxes below. Explain the connections.

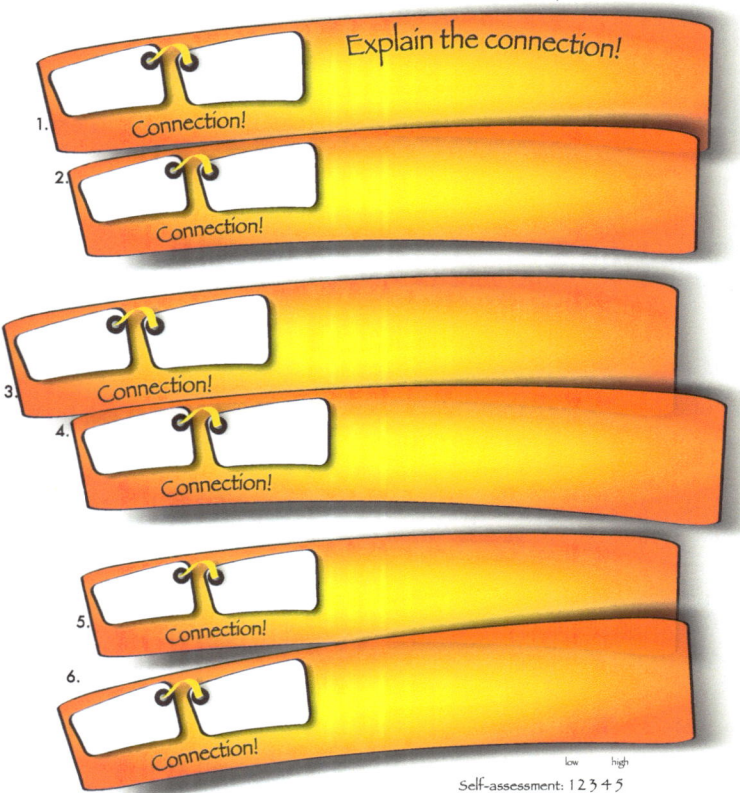

Explain the connection!

1. Connection!

2. Connection!

3. Connection!

4. Connection!

5. Connection!

6. Connection!

low   high
Self-assessment: 1 2 3 4 5

Section 4. Connection Analysis

Find six connections from Section 3. Write them in the white boxes. Think about your connections. *Why did you make these connections?* Write your reasons next to the white boxes. Be prepared to explain your reasons to your partner and your teacher.

Self-assessment: Choose what you want to assess. *How well did you do?* Give yourself a self-assessment (1 to 5).

Section 5. Partner's Connections!

Find a partner. Discuss the connections that your partner made. Write your partner's connections in the white boxes. Ask you partner why he/she made those connections. Write your partner's explanations in the space next to the white boxes.

Partner assessment: Choose what you want to assess. *How well did your partner do?* Give your partner a score (1 to 5).

Section 5. Partner's Connections!

Ask you partner about his/her connections. Write them down in the boxes below.

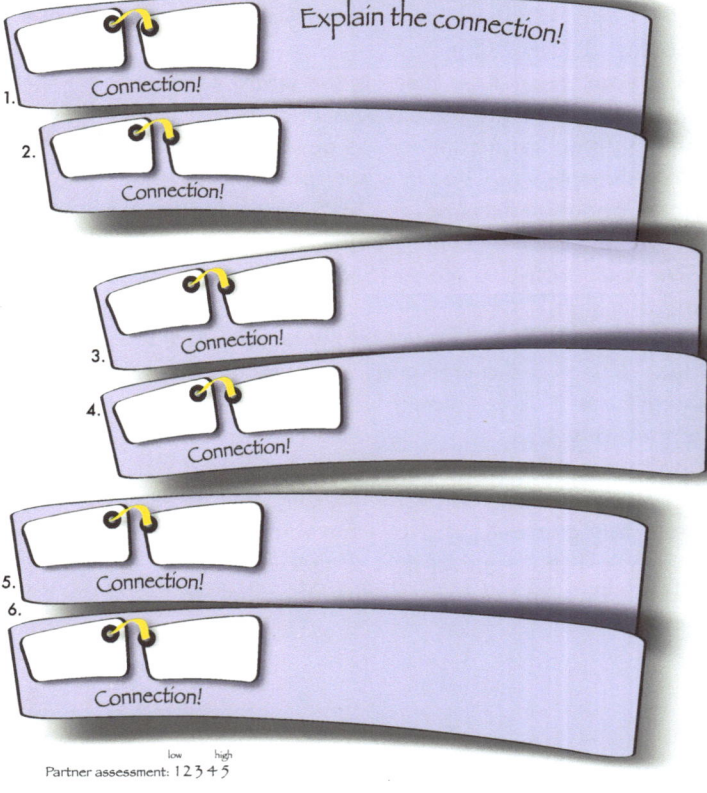

Explain the connection!

1. Connection!

2. Connection!

3. Connection!

4. Connection!

5. Connection!

6. Connection!

low   high
Partner assessment: 1 2 3 4 5

Section 6. Paragraph Writing!

Write paragraphs using your connections! Draw pictures too! Get advice.

Picture!

Connection!

Picture!

Connection!

low   high
Partner's assessment: 1 2 3 4 5
Teacher's assessment: 1 2 3 4 5

Section 6. Paragraph Writing!

Choose two connections: Think about your connections. Draw two pictures about them. Write two short (3-4 sentence) paragraphs about them.

Partner's assessment: Exchange books with your partner. Choose how you want to assess your partner. *How well did your partner do?* Give your partner a score.

Teacher assessment: Show your work to your teacher. Receive assessment and paragraph writing advice.

Section 7. Better Paragraphs!

Make your paragraphs even better!

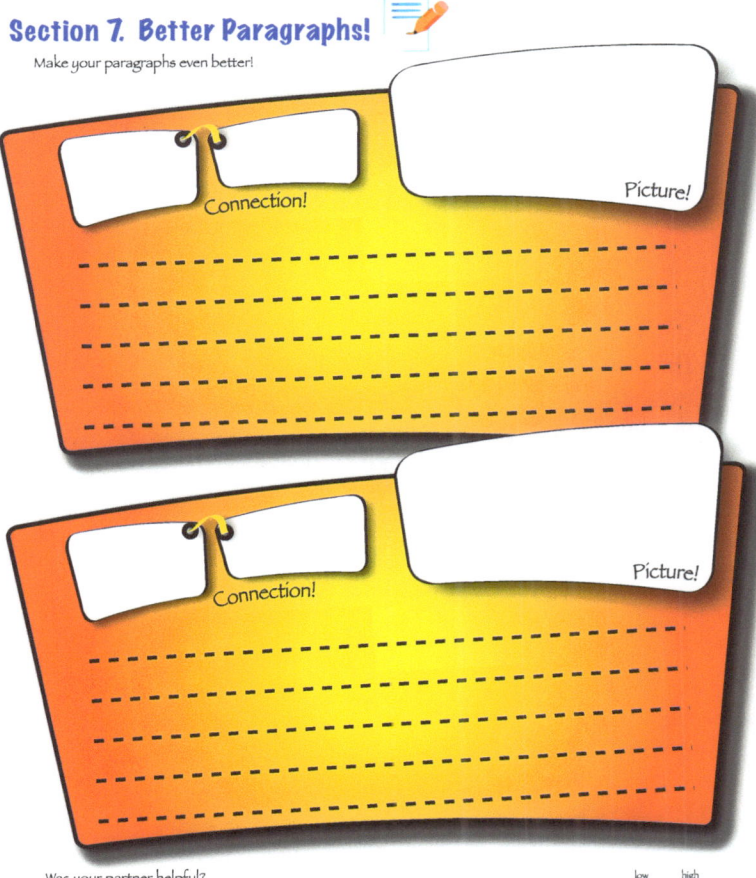

Connection!

Picture!

Connection!

Picture!

Section 7. Better Paragraphs!

Make your paragraphs even better! Think about what your partner and teacher said. Write your connections in the white boxes. Draw new pictures. Write better paragraphs!

Was your partner helpful? Think about your partner's advice. How helpful was your partner? Give your partner a score (in your own book -you don't have to show your partner this score.)

Teacher's assessment. Receive a score from your teacher. Get advice too!

Was your partner helpful?
Score your partner's help level: [1 2 3 4 5]

low   high
Teacher's assessment: 1 2 3 4 5

IMAGINATION EXPRESS

Look carefully at the picture above. Think of matching adverbs and adjectives.
Write them down. Make sentences.

Adverbs for this picture.	Adjectives for this picture.

shallow   deep
Score: 1 2 3 4 5

64

OPTIONAL: IMAGINATION EXPRESS

Look carefully at the picture. *What do you see?*
Adverbs: *Which adverbs match the picture? Write a few adverbs in the box.*
Adjectives: *Which adjectives match the picture? Write a few adjectives in the box. Use your adverbs and adjectives to make interesting sentences about the picture.*
Deep Understanding Score: *Read your sentences to yourself. Think about your sentences. Give yourself a Deep Understanding Score.*

THINK AGAIN

Think about the unit you just finished. Answer these questions.

1. What did you enjoy about this unit?

2. How can you connect what you learned to the real world?

3. What have you become interested in because of this unit?

4. Ideas for improving your skills:

low   high
Self-assessment: 1 2 3 4 5

OPTIONAL: THINK AGAIN

Think about what you have accomplished during this unit. Answer the four questions. Take your time. (Write good, well-developed answers to the questions.) Use these answers to help your future studies.

NOTES:

NOTES: